# VALLEYSPEAK

# VALLEYSPEAK

## POEMS

CAIT WEISS ORCUTT

ZONE 3 PRESS

Clarksville, Tennessee

 ZONE 3 PRESS | Clarksville, Tennessee

Library of Congress Cataloging-in-Publication Data

Names: Orcutt, Cait Weiss, 1983- author.
Title: Valleyspeak : poems / Cait Weiss Orcutt.
Description: Clarksville, Tennessee : Zone 3 Press, [2017]
Identifiers: LCCN 2017033935 | ISBN 9780990633341 (softcover : acid-free
    paper)
Classification: LCC PS3615.R37 A6 2017 | DDC 811/.6--dc23
LC record available at https://lccn.loc.gov/2017033935

**ISBN**: 978-0-9906333-4-1


Book and Cover Design by David Bieloh
Cover Art: "House of Fun" ©2012
by Sammy Slabbinck

A Tennessee Board of Regents Institution

*for Podge–*

# CONTENTS

# CALABASAS

I grow up in the valley under porn
       stars, inside cars. Mom drives us to Sunset
             Boulevard to see whores. Every whore
has a mother. Soon Mom will tell me
       about three-ways on camera, about love
             notes from convicts, how a riding crop
feels. Feelings have valleys. Soon I will drink
       to have feelings. This man Fernando is a
             shit saint; he will show me he hardly knows
this town at all. Where did saints go
       in the 90s? I will meet child welfare. They
             will pull me into trailers. Say *neglect* like a lash.
Patron saint? He'll be silent. I'll wear a gold cross
       in 1999, the year Mom divulges all her skin
             flicks. The gold cross will pink & poppy me
with rashes. Blood on bare flesh. Pelt on floor.
       It's a miracle to be born a vessel. We have so much
                         rind to burn.

# COPS & CLOUDS

Bride in white by orange
roof tiles—we bachelorette
Mom's cousins, all gams & six feet

tall. Peonies, these femmes fold
& flow in poufs. Hello late 80s
ever-prom, hello our azure pool.

My sister Podge & I worm past
their heels, their ladder legs, our heads
halfway up long tan thighs.

            The doorbell rings.

            A cop arrives.

We inspect his short shorts.
His police boombox.
We pull off our dresses,

belly-flop to blue. The pool
past our French doors occludes
the man in thong. On our backs,

            we call each cloud

            by its animal song—

suspended in
our tiny chlorine sea,
our wilderness of sky.

## ENCINO HILLS

Broken neck of bird of paradise, yuccas
slit & all the tiny blown to pieces bits of bottle

brush fluff our backyard. Our yardman's name
is Alfred. Our housekeeper is Gladys. She crossed

into America in the trunk of a car. We are two young
white sisters rolling *rrrs* to become her as she plugs

in our night lights. We eat popsicles
poolside. We hear Gladys' language, learn stories

from Mom. There once was an angel
on our street. She stole shipping rights

in the Atlantic, made millions, but then,
didn't want it enough. Now she sleeps

on the driveway of a curled street in Encino
near the Gelsons where the Jackson Five babies

were born. *American Heiress.* She is real. Mom
says, *Come live with us.* Or: Mom puts the strap

with the ball between her teeth. Or: Mom
shakes the capsules into her palm. Or:

Mom's dad calls her *Potato* as the orb
Valley sun slides itself into bed. Sixty

vicodin. Gladys calling her *angel.* Alfred
appears when no other men show,

explains the limbs of all our trees are dying.
He is kind. We girls see the lines the earth kissed

into his face. The bottlebrush sheds blood-drops
all the same. Or maybe, Mom shouts through our canyon,

*I am not even beginning to understand.*

# THE MILLION PERVERTS

*We realized that when there are 700 million porn rentals a year,
it can't just be a million perverts renting 700 videos each.*
— "one of the porn people" interviewed by Frank Rich, 2001

Porno hill in
porno ivy off porno
exit, 101.

Sex has a color
scheme: beige, blush
pink, purple

bruise, gonzo
jelly. Mom buys Thin
Sandwich

Wonder
bread. I am A B or C
girl. A: my call,

but B or C:
I take it where they say
I take it.

Famous Male
Journalist interviews
Leading Lady

Porno Star.
His verdict: *She doesn't
know she's*

*naked.* Says
Journo-Male: porn
people have

*no sense
of humor.* O. A B C
women raised

me laughing
at a cock. Journo,
research deeper

inside prick
-ling violence. Spit
on yourself, then

raise a child.
A B C women run
households, girl

scouts, studios,
this town. What Lions
gate? What Para

mount? Think
about, around & in it.
Think more

pink, more side
ways. Have you ever
banged your way

up & out
a valley? Were you
laughing

then? All A B C
D E F G women know
they're naked,

& why
it pays. We use all parts
of the pig to make

the sausage.
It tastes so good you'd
never know

that meat
is the inside of a creature
turned out,

the muscles rippling
within something still
achingly, defiantly

alive.

## SPRING IN GENESTA

Mom says better be sexy, not pretty,
introduces us sisters as The Whore
& The Nun. I'm The Nun. Convent City.
We don't catch Mom's meaning, but more & more
I suspect that my sister is winning.
At twelve, I shove thick Abbaye de Belloc
into my mouthhole, tuck Ruffles, Ring Dings
in my bed. My sister finds a crop top
like some people find Jesus. Like I find
Mom in EMT arms carried outside.
Like the note she will leave me saying *I
had to get out.* Of her body? I try
          not to freak when I bleed all my lining.
          Red porcelain: my cells divide, divining.

## DON'T FORGET! THIS MOTHERS' DAY

One seethes herself into a sluice. Shoots daydream out a luge.
Silicone, motorboat, Hang Hole bags. One is just your mother.
Ding Dongs at snack time in the Day-Glo kitchen. Remember
your childhood—the good one? One recites Faust, slices
rivers in her thigh. Drinks. Drinks. Remember the flash flood?
Water round your ankle? Round trees? You are number one,
but one is tous Max Factor, tous Chanel. Another one is just
a Jew. One a dairy farmer in NJ. Where is this place,
NJ? One hacks up piglets, communes & fingers. Blood-
stone beads, garter lace. Remember how reeds grow?
Punching soil. One raises a playboy toddler, husband blast
by a torpedo. Everyday. Everyday. One is the mother you keep
becoming. Remember the drained waterways? The L.A. River
is a coffin. Bone-dry & full of stones. Mothers, bloody water,
droughts & droughts & days. One & one & one, daughters all
we hack our veins for answers, Clorox our memories. I remember
nothing.

## WELCOME TO THE MOMENT

in which I tell you I am all right, *totally* all right, with not having     a child.

My family's women say they'd have bet *barren* if they had their chips back.

My lover & I hoard coins every day.

There are so many things left to regret but no one regrets the things they haven't done, yeah?

Like hard drugs (though I do not regret that one time with opium) or bad men (& I do not regret the biter who blared FOX News when he came).

No, my lover & I see the endgame. My lover & I cash our balance.

No, my lover has fifty days sober. We have ten years as a couple, a long throw of the die. He's not proposed.

No, I count every card in this deck.

No, my lover drinks me in with clear eyes, tells me *I can't imagine a baby with you.* Tells me *I can barely take care of myself.*

No, I swaddle my brain in clean linen, baby wipe the *real* from each tender pink lobe. O this will work out eventually, I coo. You me baby, I sing every night.

My twelve-step friends say: *love an addict from a distance.*

My lover keeps a hand on my belly, his eyes off the bottle. I keep his words from creeping into my core. No, baby. No. Baby.

I birth a phantom, make it crawl cross our floors.

# CHARITY

We go to Venice Beach with cupcakes for Easter.
     We are not Christian, but Mom decrees
we will give the homeless baked goods today.

We are girls, chiffon & basket-weaved, flowered
     up & flush. Mom is in her mango cashmere
twinset second-hand. We leave the car in the all-day

lot, pastel-clad, veering towards the waves. I have half
     a dozen cupcakes. One man sleeps a yard from me.
*Well,* Mom whispers. *Go make his day.*

The man has a beard & a belly & a growth
     on his neck. He has a bottle of something gold
by his side. Mom had two Buds before we drove here, but her eyeliner

is perfect. Her lipstick is on straight. *Happy,* my mouth leaks out.
     *East—*      His eyes open.      I run.
Podge & I have no idea how thin the icing is

between us & this man. How fridge-crisp our lives are kept
     by the cold sprinkling of cash. We know the beach man
was born into the wrong family. In ours, you can bounce

from each drop. Our money, good money, crooks its fingers
     in our breakdowns. Pulls our family's addicts back up
by our teeth. Every time she is asked, Mom hands out

spare change. *How did you get here?* I want to know.
     I don't understand yet that our genes helix addiction.
I don't understand I am seeing us, minus trust funds.

I stay silent, & Mom says: *You still have cupcakes*
     *in your basket.* I stay silent, & Mom says:
*Give more.*

## ODE TO THE GOLDEN

weeds outstretched, up, up into gray. Dawn's sky is constant in its pregnancy. Here it frosts in the mornings. Here mountain lions stalk. The family sleeps beneath terracotta but even the young one stirs when the fog rolls across the earth like a cold hand on a waist, the sharp howl of the coyotes. Barely wild, the family sleeps under polyester, a chintz print, but dawn cracks & soon the father flips his body like an egg. The mother, across the front lawn, in her own bed in the guesthouse, has dropped her glasses on the floor, flailing in the night. She dreams she is the captain of the worst disasters. Alien spaceships. The Axis Powers. PTA. She will stay asleep, but soon the ooze of sunup is seeping through the blinds, clambering through door cracks. The father stands, showers, dresses, pours tangerine juice in a thimble glass, takes a fingernail shard of Prozac, sips & swallows backed by light. *Such light!* he thinks. *Such quiet.* Right here inside the gold-calf-called-sunrise, a chalk-lined circle, his lonely morning, here he loves this life.

# PORTRAIT OF FAMILY WITH LANA TURNER

Mom claims tracking shot, ash blonde hair & breakfast
    nook. The ghost of Lana Turner flips & bevels

here/gone/here. Hollywood's a swinging door
    for the debutanted, loosed-up angels, smudged

-out stars. O brave new world of white girls
    made                blondes.

Ms. Lana wriggles down our hall. Mom came west
    to be an actress, now kicks a hole through

plywood doors. Our father surfs. He stays on-call.
    Gladys our El Salvadorian housekeeper stops by.

She wants no part of *gringa* madness. *Mujeres*
    *locas*. But still she feeds us hotdogs, drives us

through a canyon bust open as a jaw.
    What was California before the blondes

took root? My hair, lighter than Gladys',
    but worlds darker than Mom's, tangles every night.

Gladys pulls the comb. Lana flips
    the light switch. Mom sunbursts to painkillers,

platinum. Podge & I linger outside our home, count UFOs,
    sing with Gladys to Selena's *bidi bidi*

*bom bom*. We watch Lana's postman ring twice—
    see her sex, small violence. The housewives'

little trick. We wait for Mom like we wait for aliens.
    Lipstick rolls across linoleum. Lana—

is that you? Gladys leaves. Doris arrives.
    Doris leaves. Carmen arrives. Carmen leaves.

The camera climbs. There is a Gladys
    in the kitchen. Two girls hiding

in her skirt. There is a Mom with cigarillo.
    Men & men & women—borders, bodies,

double lives. *Murder* is such a flimsy word
    for editing. *Mother* is such a flimsy word

for the pack it takes to raise a child.
    *Housekeeper* for the women stashed

under-the-table, inside-the-trunk, coyote-run
    past barbed-wire, stars. Half-mothers carved

from history like organs. *Olvídala.*
    Whiteness, our city bends naked, bleaches

its blood. Lana struts as Mom sleeps in our hills.

# NORTHRIDGE

Bedrock—we say it like some families say Our Father.
      *This house is built upon bedrock.* We live in fault
land, on fault lines. My best friend from sixth grade
      will tell me about *touching* & her mother's
boyfriend, but not yet. Now we lie

side by side in her twin bed. The spine
      of the townhouse has snaked
out its own back. We will learn soon about snakes
      who eat their own tails. Males who consume
their young whole. Chronos ate as many gods

as he could fit in his gut. Here in Northridge
      my sixth grade boyfriend dated my best friend
first. She broke him in. The mother's boyfriend will break
      into her bedroom, tell her *no one needs to know*
because *no one believes* anyway.

No one believes. We sleep on bedrock, a whole
      Valley built of stone. I keep throwing
pebbles of asphalt, tiny moons, in the river, hear them clink
      across concrete. Some day, we pray, even this
will be swallowed by rain.

# WHAT BLOOMS

Our father buys lilies at Casa de Flores, but in Noir,
        men hold scarves in their laps. Have daughters hot
as greenhouses. Daughters peeling

their clothes off like leaves. Our father buys flowers
        because he's messed up. Invited
Mom's least favorite of all his friends home.

Podge & I learn from Mr. Florin
        not to trust an unbudding. Not to trust
an eros lily slipping out of its sheath.

March comes. My sister maroons herself
        on a foam float in our pool. All sand's
concrete. Encino Ocean. She is pure tan California

pre-tween. Mr. Florin tells our father
        he buys young girls in Thailand.
Our father tells Mom, who spits beer

through her teeth. *All men are monsters.*
        Not all monsters
are men. We study Loch Ness

in third grade. Podge & I whisper *Nessie lives*
        *in our pool late at night.* She swims
in sapphire, in five hundred watt bulbs. The pool light

& the moon. The moon & Mr. Florin.
        A twelve-year-old child.
Mom writes a thick note with Sharpies.

*My girls*—the note starts. Everything pale
        gets pressed flat at some point.
All monsters aren't monsters.

Podge floats off
        to deep space. Mom uncaps
one pill bottle, then another. Mr. Florin takes the red-eye.

Our father carries a port glass to the pool outside.
        Mom swallows. Mom
swallows. Nessie swims out to flower pots

beyond the light switch. All girls skinny
        dip late at night. Mom will recover,
go under, recover. Mr. Florin flies back in the fall.

Our moon grows red. Our pool light burns out.
        Our valley clings tight to each petal
as each petal flutters stupidly, time-stamped & silent,

in no way prepared for the dark.

## SOUNDSTAGE, FEATHER

Slim moment, where hope enters
            as chute of light,
one day without a drink—

now two—a year—to claim

is the prelude to losing, I know.
            I've known losing & once
considered myself best

lost. Still—strange beam—how

could I see a spotlight unless
            I stood there in the dark?
This is, then, where life

(re)starts. Darkness: a universe

dust-clothed, the lone mind's secret
            hum. *Be afraid, I know your
story*. I admit this life

its imperfections. I am profoundly

imperfect, but I am not alone
            in that. I run my fingers
up & down my human seam.

So what?

Hope wingspans, flies lumens
            through a dusty office, a super
market, a parlor scene—brave new, then landing

in my palm. Bright

universe, chiaroscuro, a fabric scrim,
            one feather gliding
through sunlight—for me—

## PHASES OF MOON

My father fills the red plastic boat with sugar, tap water.
Sits in his deck chair. Plays flute. I count the dots
of his hummingbirds. Declare them a hundred.

A murder. A clan. Aqua & pink glinting by. Junky-
eyed slurs in flight. My father's music lances the fat
end of day, sluggish rise of late afternoon moon.

Nearly a million. A cosmos. Time moves forwards
& backwards but we can only blame backwards.
I learned that once & again & again. The birds fly,

      land, sip, fly.
           I am (not)
                 my future yet.

# VALLEYSPEAK

# TOMORROWLAND

Mom takes me & my sister to Disneyland, pays us
    a quarter each when we spy the Matterhorn's peak.

The matter of our father's memory keeps sneaking in.
    The Alzheimer's threat—Old Father Time with a Taser,

no cane. Our grandfather died pissing himself between neighbors,
    unable to find a way home. No memory & wandering while my father

called Grandma, heard how death toddled the suburbs of Florida's
    hard sun. *I wish,* our father had chanted, *there was more*

*I could do.* My sister & I soar in Dumbos. We are small enough
    to believe a Disney princess is real. Mom can't let Sleeping

Beauty lie without sniping:
    *She's your father's perfect woman. Isn't that sick?*

I like Dopey. For a while he has been my invisible
    friend. Mom is Funny, or Angry. Our father is Sleepy, Forgetful,

*Workaholic,* Mom tells us. *My housekeeper,* she jokes,
    *is the closest thing to a husband I'll ever get.*

I throw pennies down the well just to hear Snow White's echo.
    I imagine her red bow trapped beneath the coin-sorting screen.

Mom tells us our father said he'd kill himself with painkillers
    before getting Alzheimer's like Grandpa. He was the one parent

we thought we could trust. Now daily, I check our father's memory.
    How close to his slow death are we? The castle we visit shrinks

inch by inch every year. *Girls, you can't depend on anything,*
    Mom tells us. Soon I see over the water in the submarine ride.

Mom recites each blank space my father provides. Each recital,
    awards ceremony he does not make. She makes them all.

She is the whole show whether he shows or not.
        Alzheimer's. In my mind, there is Mom. Mom. Mom.

Mom. Our housekeeper on weekdays. Hardly ever my father.
        As if he parceled forgetting us so we were already

half-gone. We un-remember him too.
        We stay too late at the Main Street Parade, turn

into back alleys that aren't on the map.
        Every character removes their heads, unzips their backs.

*Girls, don't look*, Mom forces her hands over our eyes, spins us
        around faster than teacups. *Whatever you think you saw,*

*just forget.*

## ROAD ATLAS: ONE

We pile the pill bugs into the backseat of Mom's car,
          call the insects Miranda, Consuela, Rachel, all girl names
for small creatures who duck, cover, roll. In school we learn not
          to be violent—only boys are violent. We learn earthquakes

are *no joke, kids*. When the alarm sounds we duck,
          cover, roll. Mom says, *Girls, we are going away.*
*It's about time to be free.* We drive north & then more north.
          CA, OR, WA up to where my sister attracts

Jesus. He lives near Vancouver & sells cassette tapes.
          Mom buys the full set, lets Podge play them while our car
walks on water via ferry. Mom remains unreligious but Jesus
          is gorgeous & our father is gone. Only the pill bugs

drive with us &, now, Jesus' songs. Moving on, we meet men
          with guns & burst capillaries, men manly enough to make
even Mom break a sweat for our culminating sins: trespassing, horse-
          nabbing, skinny-dipping, small theft, & teaching two girls

there is no difference except power between what's called
          right & what's called wrong. Wasp-bitten & welt-ridged, we tuck
into Mom. Our pill bugs break loose. Miranda, Elaine... A hippie tells me,
          *Never own anything that isn't calling your name.*

& then: *Never own anything.*

                                                                    Mom—


There is no world beyond us, this trip, your low voice.
          I am the pill bug in your Honda, our tiny car
on your roadmap. I am that *anything* calling.
          You own me already.

We duck, cover, roll home.

## RESEDA

Before we know we are rich, we go to Poor
School. Concrete fields in a parking lot,
we are elementary planets, all, orbiting
a 7-11, its cheeseburgers the sun, their molten
yellow glaze.

Mom says,

       *Heiresses can do better*

*than that.*

The last time we drive there I am eight, Podge
is six. Mom takes us the back way by the train
tracks where no trains run, past the poorly lit
costume shop with Sexy Doctor-Nurse play
suits we *Do Not*

*Touch. Adults*

       *Only.* By this route, we pass

the best part—

a brown yard with an iron sculpture. Half-man
half-fowl, all nude. We name him Wiener Bird
& so I choose to care for him. His wings
extended, his chest rain-worn, my Bird has no
family. He has

no home,

       no Mom, no Podge, & every

morning

drive I whisper, *Here, you can have mine.*

Mom tells me I know her better than anyone.
*You are my soul mate*, she whispers one night.
It is my job to keep this family safe. I hold
my breath

over train tracks.

      A social worker was sent

to my classroom

last week. *You can tell me anything, honey,*
*about your parents.* Stranger, please.
I know my world, how to guard it. You do not
ever stand naked, wings spread, on the street.
Even clothed, it is unsafe to be anything
but iron.

I will never

      unlearn

how to hide.

## SHE SWALLOWS STONES & VICODIN

Nothing very dangerous has happened to us lately.
How might you explain that? – I explain that, L.A. River,
as Mom's seltzer-bleached sobriety.
Sober as a Mom can get, shut house, shut liver,
what joyrides swell your belly, L.A. River?
—If life tributaries me to her & her to me,

we are dull now, drained girls/women
once Slut, Nun, Mom, now parched frieze.
*I might as well kill myself*, she whispers, white
fisted, dry drunk death on dewy breeze,
singing ambulance, stained nightgown, pale knees
carried. Drowning?—You don't enable drunks, L.A. River.

Not like me. I pray for Mom to lean
rosacea cheek upon my shoulder. L.A.
River, fill your basin & wash this fiend,
wipe red from wrists with thieved
ground water. Please. L.A. River
—she is an ocean I can't swim in.

# QUICK SKETCH OF A HUMAN HEART

*I see you're studying the human heart,*
our father moves to dining room table.
Here my books are spread. Here my church
is laid. *Let what I learn matter,* I pray
each day. But today—O new day—our father
takes my notebook, rips out a page. *Show me
a ventricle! Some pulmonary veins! Can you locate
an aorta?* I smell Old Spice & his toothpaste,
Tropicana afterglow. What god stoops

       for homework? I recite every lesson
       I've ever heard. *Valves are the size of half*

*dollars. A blue whale's heart weighs fifteen
hundred pounds. I know in the earthquake
you came to save me. No one else would have
checked. I love you.* I don't say the whole speech, just
the valve & whale. What does our father know?
How to bring back the dead? Or just when best
to leave them? *Arrhythmia is when the heart
beats an abnormal rhythm.* Our father hands me

       his sketch. *I know you'll ace this.* He backs away.
       *You're like me, kid. You can hold the world inside.*

I can hold the whole world.
       I make a map from his drawing.
           All the gapes & escapes in one heart.

# TO THE LOCH NESS

Or more specifically its monster,
　　　　long tail whisper
in our swimming pool: in a valley
　　　　girl's mind. Girls, mind
the valley,

its cunts, the dark water,
　　　　Jurassic trees' sweep
late at night—Riot
　　　　Grrrl Loch Ness is churning.
We towel off, full

frothed, Sweet Valley
　　　　Ophelias, who haven't quite
drowned. No, we float by the usual
　　　　suburban fiends—the parent
who uses, the lover/

aggressor who lays  in wait
　　　　by the lockers, the janitor
who slithers, *hey girls show me*
　　　　*your tits.* A Yale interviewer rubs
his thumbs under bra

straps, puts his hands on my hips.
　　　　From our pool an L.A. River
is beginning to course. Podge emerges
　　　　from pre-teen, grows up heart-first
like some women

just have to do. She loves a man
　　　　who tries to kill her.
She slits his face with fingernails,
　　　　tries to kill him back. We fish
whole futures from stank

waters, keep monsters fed. Shelter
          perversion. Mostly others'. Sometimes
ours. We say nothing's dead that couldn't once
          be living. Every single fossil out there
once managed to survive.

# LINEAGE

My grandmother the model did not suffer
    the supernatural, or God, or pianos
    or all bourgeois things,

but the blood in the glass was enough
    to stop her from having the abortion.
    Instead she kept the fetus, a little worm

inside her. *Less terrifying*, she told me
    over steak tartar. My lover & I
    want travel but that night my brain unpacked

its lobes like a suitcase (or a stroller)
    because what would it be like to hold one small *us*
    in my hands?

Mom renounces: *the drinking, depression,*
    *your father*—the whole trip—except for *you girls.*
    A woman is whole only when she's

with child. A woman pumps a watermelon
    out the width of a coin. A woman is whole
    only when she leans forward. It is selfish

to not have a child. It is selfish to have.
    I am selfish. We/he/she are selfish.
    My lover takes beef pink as white infants,

sears it, both sides. *We never travel,*
    I want to tell him. My body's a ghost ship,
    a red moon, a blood glass. Our shelter, a torn

tent, a white flag, a time-blind dissolving,
    the whole empty
    night sky.

# ROAD ATLAS: TWO

We dug them up from backyard soil—
      turned over rocks, tipped up

their homes. We are the earthquakes,
      we girls, drafting our dream team

of pill bugs. We don't give a shit
      who dies in this game.

Our pets, small minions.
      We pile our pill bugs

in Payless shoeboxes. We paint stripes
      with nail polish, let them learn

as the varnish seeps in
      how it feels to poison oneself

into *tame*. We take them into Mom's car.
      *To Canada!* Mom rallies. No men

on this trip. Just a beat-up leather bag
      of backseat car games & these bugs,

our earth-holders. They tuck their last mites
      of soil in their bellies as they roll.

*What if our world*
      *were as simple as that?*

I don't say. We get in the car.
      Mom pulls out from Hayvenhurst

to the wide stream, the real river, the 101
      Freeway. Girls, bugs, we pummel

ourselves up the coastline, un-being
      a kept thing. We keep all our legs

in our stomachs. Our homes
        burying deeper inside

as we go. What a race
        of pretending,

to think anyone gets away.

# NO PROBLEMO

when grade school takes *Colonial Week!*, rebrands it *California Days!*, saying *We,* in their best white protestant accent, in polos, salmon chinos, *must celebrate our distinctive past.* I am last

wave, one of the old-school forced to read *The Scarlet Letter,* respond to Goody, weave wool on looms. Podge is younger, *la nueva tendencia*: Spanish skirts & mission bricks, or even:

the Tongva, Uto-Aztecan, absorbers of the Hokan-tongued. Once we brought Podge, August tan, down to Tijuana. Mom said: *careful or those border men will claim she's one of them.*

That October week of *California Days!*, I watch Podge cross over oak trees' roots, mortar acorns, mouth *Gabrieleño, Fernandeño, Nicoleño*, throw each round string of sounds aside. Our school

chooses her to lead its "Mission Pageant." She is a bronzer-shaded, faux-*Mestiza* starlet. A natural on the stage. Still—patience. *California Days!* can't last forever. We know how this ends.

*Viernes*, Podge plays noble savage, then virtuous ranchero bride. But soon as school breaks for the weekend the tribes all catch the flu. The missionaries pull out. Slaughter comes. Spain leaves

& Anglos swarm. Eastern traders, Midwestern men, dust-clad & digging for land, water, gold. Come Monday, our teachers start class with, *Back to Business!* Episcopalian prayers, proper

grammar, the heaving canon. They remind us to stay ever vigil— we are a valley on a hill, a wagon circled round by illegals, crack fiends, & casinos. Podge learns history is a pack of lies. I tell her

noir is everywhere. Every plot's a cover-up. We unearth the loom, place our hands on yarn. The warp & weave. Inheritance, by land & sea. The dictionary becomes our blanket, smallpoxed, homespun,

contexere. We look that up. Latin— "to weave." Warp is simpler, we are fluent:

> "that which is thrown away."

# HALLOWS

Mom's moustache is kohl-lined, clean. Our father's
a Jewish Klingon. Podge, harem floozy.
I'm a witch. I wear jeans. I don't bother.
with costumes or slashers, drugs or boozing.
Being fourteen's enough horror as is.
Mom appears: slim suit, cufflinks—a mister.
*I'd sleep with myself.* Our father thumbs his
pager. He won't put it down to kiss her.
My sister's bellybutton casts a spell
on candy-handers. O pre-teen promise.
Last night I dreamt I was a man. I fell
in love with a girl, her hair's soft blonde kiss.
       More gorgeous, my mother, cross-dressed manly,
       walks out of the house, leaving the family.

# ODE TO THE ONE GLOVE

nonstop on the radio. If it fits, the Iranian carpool mom won't drive up the driveway. Her Bentley scrapes its belly on the white family's tar. If it fits, the kids skip school for a week due to *riots*. The white family lives twenty miles from the burning— *might as well live in Canada*, the mother says. Is there even one black family living here in Encino? Jews don't count. If it fits, the children hear *violence is not the answer* looped like a noose, but they also hear *show your work*. Every calculation: *show your work*. The mother takes the children downtown during the *OJ*. The whole family has heard about Rodney King, Daryl Gates. *Can't we all just get* more gates. The children see a body dragged from a truck & smashed like a watermelon on pavement. Videos looped like a noose. If it fits. The mother in the warehouse gets the children to make tuna salad. She pulls out ten five-gallon jars of relish. The children hate relish. *So what it's not for you.* The children know OJ for: slow driving; glove jokes; the fact that he is not a juice box; the rumor he did it, but *so what it's not for you*. Once the white family got lost driving by Compton. The mother peed on a towel instead of leaving the car. The family has read *Bonfire of the Vanities*. What's urine on terrycloth. What's a glove on a black man. What's a white woman but a good excuse for lynching. But what if he didn't? Looped like a noose. The girls draw gloves in their art class. Take their hands & then trace them like bodies. Like bodies but *not* bodies. They wash their hands in the sink, play house.

## ALWAYS TELLING

                           the truth is as pathological as lying.

My fingers
        are naked. My lover swallowed my engagement ring at last call.
Now he's sober so I wait to see how he'll take me, eyes open wide in the
dark. What I'll find in his pupils: my own flaws reflected, the formerly
beer-goggled cut sharp.

My body
        isn't twenty. Big whoop but it betrays me each day. What I loved
about drinking: the infinite truths I could hold & not see. Twenty was
lying like a hot drunk on a futon, spread eagle & not giving a fig.

Love & time
        are both fuckers. I watch the women in my family age to plastic.
Perma-MILFs in veneers, they raise a glass, keep their heads above
second/third waves of feminism, decades of rock-hard nipples, bonfire
bras & the rank sell-by stamping of *A Certain Age*.

I play
        *shoot the bitch* games on my lover's PlayStation, siphon coffee
with a fervor that lights up my veins, exhale in AA meetings in church
basements with drunks, chant to dark spaces: *I am. I am. I am.* My
body: only, yet always, the cage.

My sick
        lover has ten days without whiskey, gimlet, Slow Comfortable
Screw. He tells me *it's like I can see the world clearly*. I have years I've
spent sober. I see enough to get by. It is awful/awe-filled, so much
clearness. I say nothing, watch my language as close & tight as the bottle,
line the shots up of *one day at a time*.

# FRONTIER

Mom made us matching guidebooks to Alaska,
      copied, bound in a Kinkos
            in the Valley on a school day.

We have made it. The frontier.
      Rented car & Day Four:
            Mom hides out in a Kodiak

internet café, dashes off missives
      to RootBeer, secret boyfriend,
            former country-music DJ.

RootBeer is not yet a known threat
      to our family. We drive through Denali,
            denial. I listen only & wholly

to Barenaked Ladies, press play,
      play, play. I pretend it hardly matters
            our father refuses our rotation

of sitting backseat. The only male,
      he is perpetually the assumptive
            *shotgun*. I am fourteen. Life just now grows

its big tits of *unfair*. We are here in Alaska
      on a ten-day car trip.
            In six months, she'll admit the affair.

In a year he'll sign off on divorce.
      I'll stay a virgin three years after that
            but here in Alaska

is the first place men see me,
      see my breasts orbiting within
            my galaxy of skin.

My body's the eventual
       swirling Milky Way. When a stranger
             in flannel blows a kiss on the highway,

I press one nipple to the window
       of our rented Ford Escape.
             My family drives three hours

to stare at black worms trapped in glaciers.
       We come back at twilight & walk in pairs: girls
             & grown-ups on the dock.

Between salmon dead
       & salmon dying, Mom
             holds our father's hand in the light.

It's midnight & I notice
       men & women everywhere
             flip a universe for cock.

# BULLET

You watch them from      high chairs & rocking
    horses, backseats        like gaped mouths, kid-sized
barstools. One could store    a little girl (or two)

    nearly anywhere. A closet. Can
of beer. First rule of noir: the body's the carpet. Step

lightly.        Some girls
    swivel hips like the cars snaking      Sunset
& Vine. You know    there are whole

    hindquarters of the Valley—San
Pornando—girls    can't see? Saint

of labia surgery, money    shots, camcorder. She's
    whispering.    There are more lines
than you can write down in this poem.

    On that table.  In the script.
On her face. Stardust trails

cum cocaine    & Tinkerbell.
    The clapping the audience makes    (even the dead
that's just the carpet)    is the play—

    not the light on the wall. You sleep curled, silver
spoons. Baby dolls in pink twin jars,

in Chatsworth, West Hills,    Cowboy Palace,
    airplane hangar. Tight O    of small lips
parting    small light pulsing…

    A woman's body's a shadow sewn every day—
    each stitch, a bullet—

for whom?

# VALLEYSPEAK

# THE PROPHETS

Our father sees God in the ocean, a hillside.
The divine chucks itself on his surfboard.

Science unraveled the start of the world by noting all planets are drifting away.

At fifteen, I am all girl-flesh, no faith—
O body. The globe of it expanding. New creases & out into space.

Science echoes the sprawl of a teen's day / heart / or god.
Mom wakes in-patient from an overdose,

slides out into space. I want:
the boy who plays drums to begin to painfully love me.

I drag my body to a Day of Obligation. Our father asks:
*Can you proofread my prophecy?* Something *hope.*

Something *loss.* At sixteen, I have wounds on each wrist.
Tiny stigma, stigmata. Mom comes to in a red room,

feet bent back & she's smiling.
She comes to me in the beige leather front seat of her Honda.

Mom tells: *I have a secret you can't ever share.*
All of life is the secret, & the porn, & the spheres she drives forward:

chatroom lovers, knifepoint shoes, white-knuckle sober.
As she unwinds, I fold inwards.

I fold inwards. O Earth, you are still too young & keening.
You do not know yet how to swallow the universe without tasting.

# ODE TO THE GLITZ

pageants, flippers & big hair. The closer to Jesus, the flippers, the poise. Pint-sized queen Ramsey, Mini Supreme. Hot topic at grade school: did the dad or didn't he? The children double-take their father, then themselves. Lot & his daughters. Basements in Colorado. What does it take to go carnal? Asphyxiation, strangulation, craniocerebral, applause. The girls don't know anyone who has been kidnapped, but the oldest daughter often dreams the youngest gets raptured by a dude in the sewers. He'll only let her go for a trade. The oldest goes back & forth, sometimes gives in. Sometimes won't. What would the father do, she begins to wonder. The father has told both girls he loves the mother best of all. Who would the mother kill to survive? They cannot *not* think of Anne Frank at this point, at least the father & the two half-Jewish daughters cannot. The mother thinks of Bertha Mason locked up by Rochester. Reader, she married him. Sets a fire anytime. No one, in this house, just for today, will get murdered; will murder. The girls hide their lipsticks ever since JonBenét's body was found. They wear sweatpants & sweatshirts, don't shower for a week. *Hide the goods*, nobody tells them. When, in the movie, Sophie chooses, the mother shouts out: *shoot them both.*

## PLAN B

Child of Lost
        Hours, Late Period Fantasia,
                blood-marked pajamas around four a.m., for you

                I still lie with eyes open, still feel
                    your breath at my back.

Lost Child, I unpackage
        one hand from the two that pray
                under my pillow. I reach down

                to my belly
                    to pretend you're

still there. But this bump's
        a burrito. Late evening
                ice cream. In the dream

                I'm not having,
                  you're older than I'm sober.

Child of Plan B
        Pills. College Condom
                Breaks. All the times I could

                have had you, but veered
                  away. My mother at thirty-one

had a first & third grader & eighteen years
        left of drunk days
                shouting        *Let's film*

                *a fairy tale.* I have no years
                  of drunk left. I left you

behind when I thought
        there'd be time.
                Even now        I have no idea

                as I move forward      how much future
                  I leave behind.

# LEPIDOPTERIST

Worm-threaded, Mom & Lara flux
in scarves, silk tops, sequins, pumps pinning
crooning twins to the stage. They bump

hips to the cardiac lab's jazz band. Beats
Per Minute. Heart Attack. Our father plays
the sax, the flute, the back-row blind spot.
For this premier performance the band scrawled

Double Bypass on the bass drum. Now each hit
summons the sirens snapping white orchid fingers
to *Smooth Operator*, crunching bones of a blues

riff onstage. That night Podge & I stay home, catch
bees. We are uninvited to the big grown-up show.
To catch bees: shove a jar around airlifted bodies,
screw the lid fast, tight, & wait. It is easy, we learn,

to drown small things in air. Every freedom we have,
we dig into. Podge discovers the deep end of the pool,
the hot ring of the stove. I discover each lobe of my brain

nobody can touch yet. Weeks later, we watch
Mom & Lara on the Beta. We wear footsies
while our bees wake up dead inside glass. I record
what it takes to have everyone want you: scarves,

silk tops, pumps, a man, a crowd & a video
recorder. To catch success: pin yourself
straight to the floor.

# RAZED

There is the earthquake, the flood, & riots.
In the beginning: the earthquake. I wake
screaming. A mirror will shatter before our
father carries me out. But Mom is safe.
Moonlit, she's first one on deck. The pool licks
her feet. Second: flood. Rain pours in our valley.
*Girls, let's take a drive.* Mom sets down beer, picks
the shortcut: Sepulveda Basin. We
all nearly drown. Soon, riots: our neighbors
lock doors, self-inflict curfews. Mom takes us
to Skid Row to share lunches, gain favor,
small talk humanity with the homeless.
      So she raised us come hell & high water—
      into godless gods, girls, L.A.'s daughters.

## ONE OF TWO PARTIES

You're one of two parties hiding in your bedroom, one
of two girls born of the Beauty Descendant
& a Nice—if Lapsed—Jew: there is an agreement

              between your tall gods, those two afore
                named. It is not fair or equitable.
                It is court approved. You will stay

with your father. Mom buys a white house,
eats Puffa rice, invites RootBeer, her lover,
up from San Deegers, throws mattress

              & serape like woodchips on the floor.
              Nice if Lapsed burns pork chops.
              He tries his best to feed you

but *dammit girls, can't you just
keep it down?* You keep everything
down. All the snackpacks, all the times

              you hear Lapsed call Descendant
                *filthy whore* in his deckchair
              by the pool below your window.

All the plush wedding fantasies
other girls your age are having—
you'll have none, zilch, zip. Zero

              babies will be born from your
                loins, swear to night sky,
              to stork, sperm, & Gabriel.

Parents are children enough.
They sign, both parties, kicking
& screaming in a sad room on a sad

              dotted line.

## ODE TO THE PAPASAN

nest chair, the one the mother & father hauled into the house from the incense & raffia of their past. Ode to their past. It is quite gone now. The daughters can't fathom. Ode to the Washington Mall protests, the doobies, the peace doves, the Majorcan coast. One day the family shuts itself in a beige room, pulls down the blinds. The parents set up a slideshow. Kenyan safari. Aspen's slopes. The daughters can't focus. Instead they start dancing, letting the projection bathe them in yellow, purple, blue, the blurred & pulled shapes of impossible parents. Their parents' impossible youth. One day the father will explain Plato's caves to the daughters, how nothing is what people believe it should be. The mother & father & daughters all fit inside the papasan, but they will not forever. The parents pause on one image— cityscape, dark horizon—& abandon slide clicker. Hand in hand, they walk into the light stream, let the images blind them. Hand in hand, they walk up to their daughters & dance.

## DOUBLE INDEMNITY

I am the dictaphone Mom confesses in,
our father's corpse

dropped on the tracks &/or shot at twice
in the parlor,

the anklet that cuts his skin like red
lipstick cuts

a woman's face. In these films
Mom has a gash

& a snatch—but who is lighting her match?
RootBeer? My sister

is Lola, carwasher, the women who keep
interrupting

Mom in the drugstore as she pivots
in mink, plotting

to kill. I am worried about her
cigarette. Will I light it?

In these films the credits run first. Soon
Mom is no longer

breathing. I am playing, replaying
each scene past its

climax. Like I've never seen burning.
Like I've never learned

cigarettes are all ash
by the end.

## SINGLE KINGS OF THE VALLEY

Our father becomes one. Barrel-Chested
with Longboard seeks Mate. King Father
is dating. Long live the King. He asks out

colleagues, neighbors, strangers he meets
at Spazzio's Jazz Night, Zuma Beach.
He dates the moonlight, his reflection,

the long ago that got away. The King says
*Why the hell shouldn't I get what I've longed for?*
Nip waist, taut tum. *Where is she?* His exile

from the good stuff. *You girls can't imagine
the pain you'll cause men.* Nope, we don't
& we can't yet but we do know the King

cannot consider us worthy. How could he?
As women, we fail him daily. Love, I'm learning,
is peeling your mind from your body, throwing

one or both sad sacks of self out to sea. Love
is blood & our father. I give no inch. I judge
the world from the margins of diaries. *Men*

*are the problem with everything.* King Father
slices lemons from our lemon trees. Citrus grows
in the grove beneath my bed. Mom lived

in our guesthouse for three years before leaving.
She peeled herself slowly off his heart like a scab.
What is the point of such maiming? Now the King

isn't careful when he walks by the branches.
He barges through trees & their thorns.
King Single can't remember his heart soft

& rind-less. The new women are beautiful,

or not, or enough to get by. I watch him
take a lover. She is insane. The king peels

a lemon, lays each slice on her plate.
She requests lime. He hands us
whole fruits when we eat at the table.

He takes his longboard to the ocean,
                    kicks flat water into waves.

## HOLIDAY

We slide up to the tank
      in the Pass Christian air,
faux-phallus photo-shoot
      too good to pass up.

      RootBeer straddles the hatch
as Mom fingers the Nikon. The Nikon—
      I'd rather not see sex here, so I trace
a black camera back to Mom, a non-Mom Mom

at seventeen. Artist: what Mom once thought
      she could do for a living.
Her hair's long & I'm nothing
      yet. She, on my mind's film,

      keeps her non-Mom life dream.
Here she does not need to want to kill herself
      or sleep around. She is too young
& too not lonely for that. Snap back

to the innuendos of our real-life
      scene. She is thirty-seven & I think
incredible. Incredible our whole lives
      have nothing to do

      with the thoughts in the next brain.
Our whole lives can run out
      without touching anything real
in the people we love

except skin. I am fourteen, three years from believing
      I could really be someone
useful & another ten years from losing
      my dream if I dream

      as Mom does. If I am not just
a non-Mom future-Mom here

myself, if I get to be me, un-diverted,
my whole life. Slim chance, right? Mom asks me

to smile, puts her finger on the shutter.
          I think *these people*
*do not know me at all.*  RootBeer & I sit
          on the old tank, in separate wars.

Of course I will become her,
          if I just wait long enough.

In these photos, no one smiles,
          but then again,
in these photos, no one ever blinks.

# TARZANA

Before strip malls & golf courses, Spin
Cycle & juice
chains, there were male sex organs & one half-

man, half-ape. Race
riots in orange
groves. Here, 1990s: I call one girlfriend *yellow*

*as rice.* SoCal sun shoves melting pot
fingers into a dozen wide
girl eyes. Now one white girl friend

picks one tan girlfriend to call a *bean
burrito,* tells her she must *bag
our groceries.* One white girlfriend bleeds

through Earth Science in the backseat
of one white senior's car while he names beasts
of the field, calls his one white dick

*Rhythm Stick.* At pool parties, I tell
one Chinese-by-way-of-Mauritius
girlfriend to massage me (one white girl me)—

*because that's what you're here for.* One half-Jew
girlfriend (as Jewish as I am
but we say her Jew *hooks*

*onto her face)* will be raped
by one no-face no-home no-race-
we-know man in the bushes. One half-

Filipino-half-
Czech girlfriend will whisper
*she probably liked it.* One half-

Jew girlfriend gets locked
up in Rikers on charges of larceny
(context: cocaine). One no-

race man in the bushes skulks
back to business. One Fili-Czech girlfriend
gives blowjobs in strip malls.

One Mauritian-Chinese girlfriend shifts
poly, gets steamrolled
by chains & locked in three bedrooms. All girlfriends

who bleed in Corvettes marry
white boys: busboys, junior dentists, latter-day
architects. All live

behind gates, copper gates
of the Valley. All paint their nurseries
over jungle walls. All pray

for girl children. Girl
friends. All get every child
we all ever wanted. We promise

race is nothing. We are blind
to color, have
no shame.

We all have our child & name her—
keep naming her,  keep
naming her

*Jane.*

# SPIKE, JAVELIN, HARPOON

We finally talk babies,
        my lover & I. Him now at        three months, twenty-two days
           sober & me    twiddling fallopians   at five years,
two months & spare
                  change.        Today

he asks me    when I say   *sober time*   *is our baby*   if I'm nursing
        metaphors   (with damp   nips & cloth   naps & viscid infant
           shit—all the grossness the mommyblogs swear
I would love)                        or if I am talking
        about an actual       child.

If I would love        an actual child.

                  I am carrying a brain      & a spine
    & a howling.

I would like to declare this        a child. Drinking has turned

into a metaphor
    for living                        without.

Childlessness
is not a simple not having,        but a constant Lamaze:
        the in out—a taut   being-ness of   not having
& not having    & not having   what I already   quite literally
        haven't got.

*Of course it's a metaphor*, I tell him.   *But what would you name it?*

    *A baby?*   He tries. I can feel that. Love is   (not having)
the answer.    *Lance.*

        With a puncture, the name   —lessness   coos.

# MACERATION

Our father never forgave Mom enough to see her
so we spent my childhood all of us blind,

      hands held & circling, a family of spins.
      The thing about alcoholism is it's never one thing:

it shifts its face like a woman between waking & leaving.
Once pale, now rouged up, then smeared. It's incredible

      really, how little I've had to understand life
      to live it. I remember when I was eight

Mom's keys on the ground, our father
shouting *You are too drunk, V, to drive. Jesus*

      *Christ*. I didn't have to know anything, but HOME
      & NOT HOME & to keep the two things

apart. When the ambulance came, after she downed
all the pills, & the men I didn't know pulled her

      & the man I did know away, I slept in their bed
      as big as forgiveness, as big as the heart that would have to

forgive. I tried to sleep there alone. The bed swallowed
me whole. I should understand, then, at least some bit

      of forgiveness after sleeping a night
      in its gape. Here's what I know: wait

it out. Wait it out & you will find yourself
in the same place of transgression. It's much easier

      to forgive someone then.

# HOLLYWOOD

I Black Dahlia my mother: meaning, I dig up
      her dress, vintage yellow, that she wore in the last scene—leaving
         our father for RootBeer, the lover, bare backing on Sunset

in his Model T restored. I once played
      the patsy in this picture, but now I'm a woman—as old
         as the one I malign in my poems. How would I raise

me, she'd like to know. How would I
      raise rumors from the womb of a pool? I'm all woman now,
         but childless. I zip up my emptiness in Mom's yellow dress.

A bodybag.
      *Tag me,* I whisper, planting foot in black
         velvet heel. In every book, a girl's murdered, a dark girl

with dark hair. Some rich bitch, a blonde, dresses like her
      for kicks. I wear the dress to Musso & Frank's, the margins
         of childhood. Now, in a booth,

the *me* me smiles kindly, safe in a barren,
      retaliatory silence.
         But the *her* me—

                        *Hello, darling.*

She breaks through side seams, her/my yellow dress. I inhabit, strange
      habit, her body, right where I started. Remember the feeling of breathing
         inside her? I will never know love that consuming again—

except

      in this moment. & then—

I will zip out, leave the dress on the floor.
      Black Dahlia, Mom. Even murdered,
         we survive. Because who tells the stories, otherwise?

Who tells the ghosts how they died?

# VALLEYSPEAK

## PLAY HOUSE

Podge & I do not play house—we play
*Femme Fatale, Noir.* She tucks

 invisible guns in invisible cleavage. I cleave
open the birch tree by our double front doors, pull

 dry chunks of bark with my fingers,
tell Podge, *This is the place we will bury*

 *our husbands.* We pry smog-tongued
silk ties from Mom's closet. Podge palms the hole

 I have pried in the birch. A graveyard—
*But this is our baby,* she starts to tell me, starts to change

 the whole script. *This birch?* I have pulled
half its heart out. Damp darkness, a worm. *No,*

 *this is a coffin,* I convince her & me, or I convince
only her, or I convince no one & decide that's enough.  ※

 That's enough for us both to invisibly murder
our invisible husband, stuff him in an invisible baby,

 an invisible coffin, or a tree in the valley.
Before *Noir* & our birch games, our father planted that tree.

 He dug a hole in the sod of his new house
while Mom watched. Playing dead by the TV now, he reminds us

 about *witness.* The tree is a witness. There is always
a witness to hope. Always some damned fool. Two girls to play patsy.

 We all bury what we must bury
in our holes on the lawn.

## ACKNOWLEDGMENTS

Thank you to my parents, all of you, who are not the parents in these poems, but strong, curious, creative thinkers who gave me the confidence to write, the curiosity to learn, and the chutzpah to explore the line between imagination and truth.

Thank you Podge—I carry your heart. Thank you, Mami, for carrying mine for so long. Thank you to my fellow Golden Child of the Universe and to Moonsie, Meesh, Devon, and Jason.

Thank you to my childhood friends, who are not the friends in these poems, but brilliant, hilarious women who kept me grounded and laughing throughout all of middle school and high school. Jen, Sari, Laura, Heidi, Meredith, Sue Jean, Caroline, Raychael, Uma, my Valley Girls, I will always be grateful for who we were for one another.

Thank you to my grandparents, my cousins, my aunts, my uncles, my teachers, my peers, my students, my Caucus, my Johnnie C., my Coco, and my heartbreaks. Thank you to everyone that got away. Thank you to Jimmy, who, thankfully, stays. Jimmy, I love you more than I can say. You make my days golden, my valleys safe.

Thank you to LAMBDA, Jeannie P., and Grace.

Thank you to all at Zone 3 Press and to Douglas Kearney for selecting this manuscript for the First Book Award. Thank you to Susan Wallace for your care and guidance in making this book. Thank you to Kathy Fagan and Maggie Smith for reading countless drafts when this was just a thesis. Thank you to The Ohio State University, Kenyon College, the University of Houston, Inprint, Writers in the Schools, Sarah Lawrence Summer Writers, New York State Summer Writers, Sackett Street Writers Workshops, the 92 Street Y, and New York Writers Coalition.

Thank you to Mary Szybist, Gerald Harp, Stephen Dobyns, Frank Bidart, Henri Cole, Marcus Jackson, Michelle Herman, Honorée Fanonne Jeffers, Matthea Harvey, Natalie Shapero, Kaveh Akbar, Raena Shirali, Paige Quiñones, Janelle DolRayne, Mikko Harvey, Anthony Cappo, Rebe Huntman, Elizabeth Metzger, Catherine Pond, Trent Pollard, Jon Riccio, Megan Peak, Niki Herd, Kevin Prufer, and John Matthais for your edits and encouragements on these and other poems.

And of course, thank you thank you to the following journals, presses, editors, & readers for their keen eyes, their edits, & their encouragements:

*Boston Review*: "Frontier"
*Chautauqua*: "Charity"
*Day One*: "Welcome to the Moment"
*FIELD*: "Calabasas" & "The Prophets"
*Hobart*: "To the Loch Ness"
*JUKED*: "Lineage"
*Notre Dame Review*: "Portrait of Family with Lana Turner" & "Spring in Genesta"
*Pacifica*: "Ode to the One Glove"
*pacificREVIEW*: "Bullet," "Hollywood" & "Play House"
*Prelude*: "Reseda," "Hallows" & "What Blooms"
*Tahoma Literary Review*: "Ode to the Glitz"
*The Tishman Review*: "Spike, Javelin, Harpoon"
*Tupelo Quarterly*: "Encino Hills," then titled "Vanderbilts"
*Two Peach*: "Northridge" & "Ode to the Golden"